HOW COMPUTERS WORK

Steffi Cavell-Clarke & Thomas Welch

COMPUTERS AND <CODING>

KidHaven
PUBLISHING

Published in 2019 by KidHaven Publishing, an Imprint of Greenhaven Publishing, LLC
353 3rd Avenue, Suite 255, New York, NY 10010

© 2019 Booklife Publishing

This edition is published by arrangement with Booklife Publishing.

Written by: Steffi Cavell-Clarke & Thomas Welch
Edited by: Kirsty Holmes
Designed by: Danielle Jones

Cataloging-in-Publication Data

Names: Cavell-Clarke, Steffi. | Welch, Thomas.
Title: How computers work / Steffi Cavell-Clarke & Thomas Welch.
Description: New York : KidHaven Publishing, 2019. | Series: Computers and coding | Includes glossary and index.
Identifiers: ISBN 9781534527089 (pbk.) | ISBN 9781534527072 (library bound) | ISBN 9781534527096 (6 pack)
Subjects: LCSH: Computers--Juvenile literature. | Computer science--Juvenile literature.
Classification: LCC QA76.23 C38 2019 | DDC 004--dc23

IMAGE CREDITS

Cover – izabel.l, I000s_pixels, Macrovector, danjazzia. 5 – hanss. 6 – Sudowoodo. 7 – Macrovector, OmniArt. 8 – Pogorelova Olga, Maksim M,
32 pixels, Dacian G. 9 – mamanamsai, Faith Nyky. 10 – Sudowoodo, Kit8.net, Hasik-ioj, SofiaV. 11 – Jane Kelly. 12 – Sudowoodo. 13 – Sudowoodo,
filip robert. 14-15 – Succo Design, Scratch is developed by the Lifelong Kindergarten Group at the MIT Media Lab. See http://scratch.mit.edu.
16 – denk creative, A_KUDR, Sudowoodo. 17 – Top Vector Studio. 18-19 – Shai_Halud. 20-21 – MilkyM. 22 – Igogosha, RinArte, Inspiring.
23 – Oxanne, Sudowoodo.

Printed in the United States of America

CPSIA compliance information: Batch # BS18KL: For further information contact Greenhaven Publishing LLC, New York, New York at 1-844-317-7404.

HOW COMPUTERS WORK

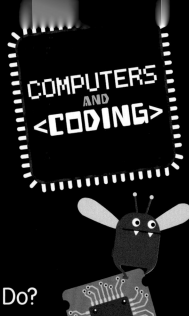

COMPUTERS
AND
<CODING>

Words that look like **this** can be found in the glossary on page 24.

WHAT IS A
COMPUTER?

A computer is a **machine** that can be taught to do something by itself. Computers do not have brains like us. They cannot think or have ideas, but they can follow **instructions** and do lots of useful things.

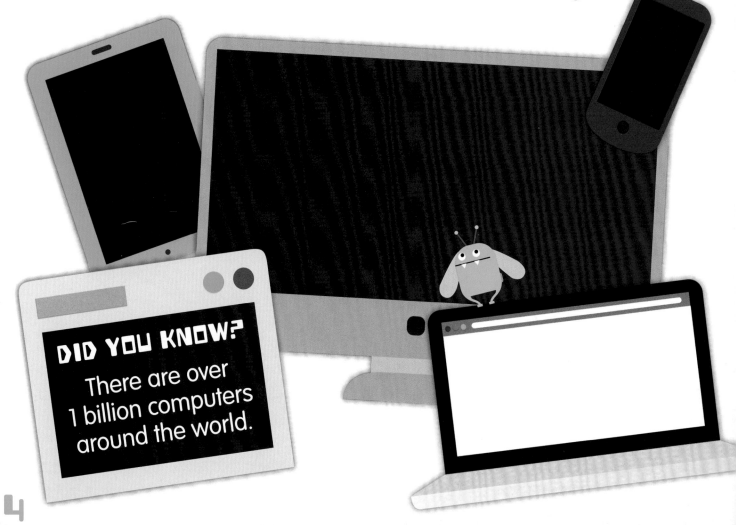

DID YOU KNOW?

There are over 1 billion computers around the world.

A computer is made up of lots of different parts that have their own special jobs.

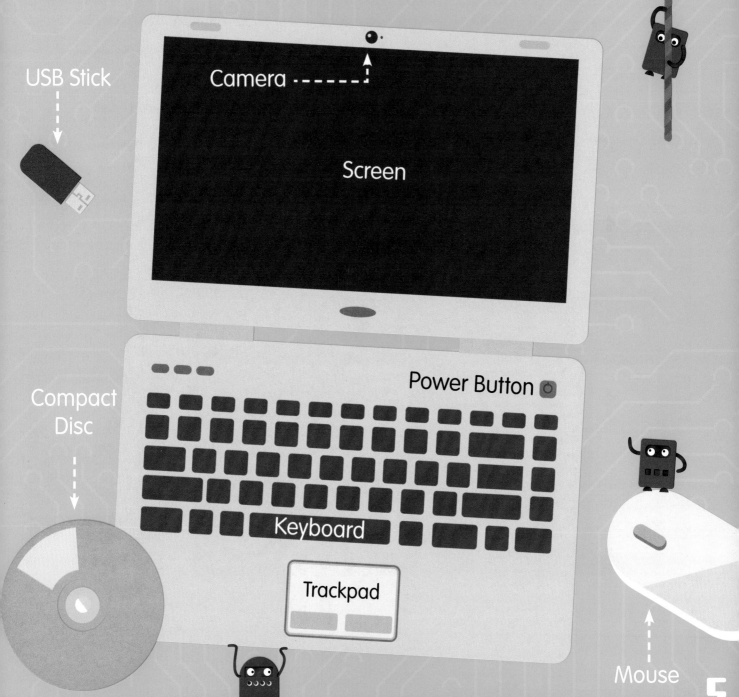

USB Stick

Camera

Screen

Compact Disc

Power Button

Keyboard

Trackpad

Mouse

5

MODERN COMPUTERS

The first computers were the size of a large room and used lots of **electricity**. These computers were mostly used to help solve math problems.

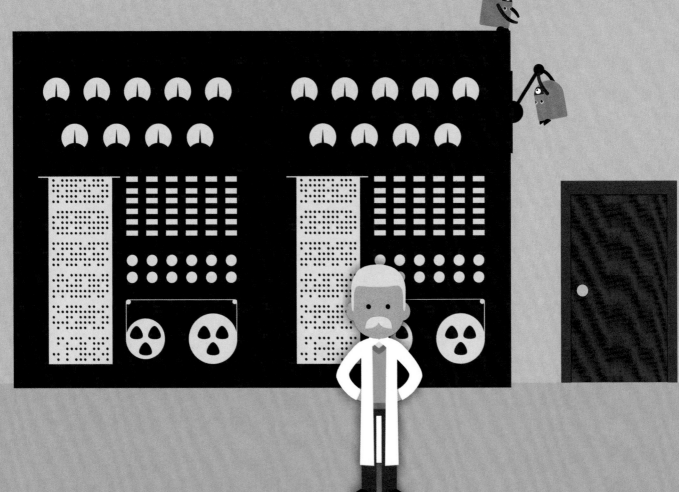

Today, computers are used all around the world. **Modern** computers are a lot smaller and can **perform** many jobs at once.

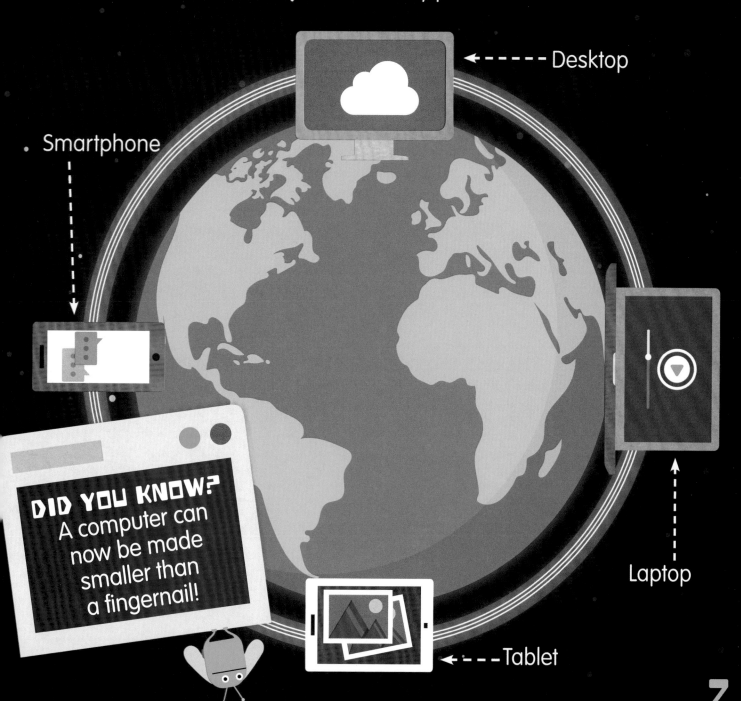

Desktop

Smartphone

Laptop

Tablet

DID YOU KNOW?
A computer can now be made smaller than a fingernail!

COMPUTER DO?

From telling the time to sending rocket ships into space, computers can do many different things. There are lots of computers hidden inside everyday objects, like washing machines and traffic lights.

Computers can help you to do many different things.

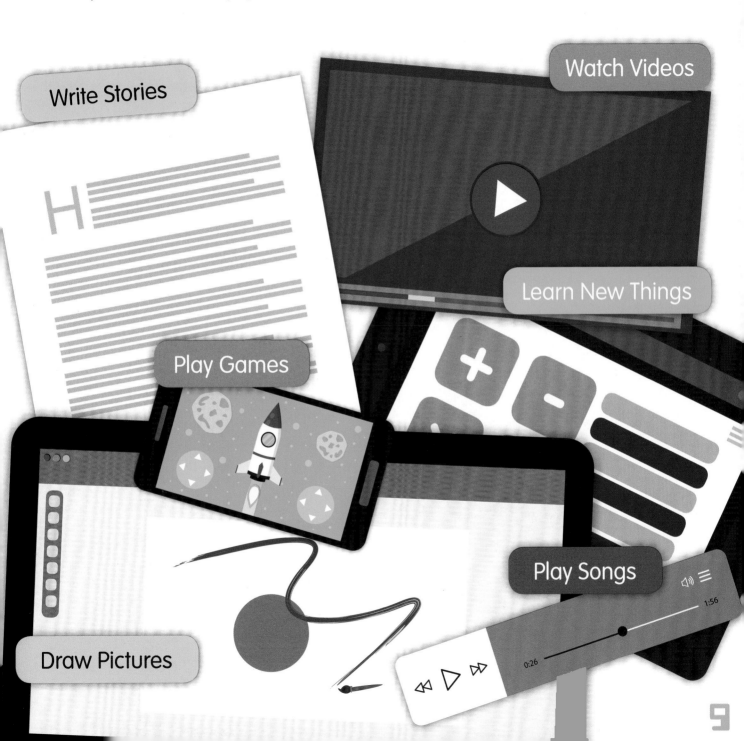

Write Stories

Watch Videos

Learn New Things

Play Games

Play Songs

Draw Pictures

USING
COMPUTERS

We are surrounded by **technology**. Many people use a computer at least once a day.

School

Home

Work

Using a computer can be fun and it can make day-to-day jobs a lot easier. Computers are useful in all sorts of places. They help in schools, hospitals, and airports. They also help us to **communicate** with other people.

HOW DO COMPUTERS WORK?

Different parts of a computer help it do different things. Some parts store information, and other parts let us see and hear information.

OUTPUT DEVICES
Parts of the computer that display or **emit** information, such as a computer screen.

CENTRAL PROCESSING UNIT (CPU)
The part of the computer that follows instructions.

MEMORY
Where the computer stores **data**.

INPUT DEVICES
How the computer receives information, such as a keyboard.

Information is put into a computer through an input device. The information is sometimes stored in the computer's memory, or it will be processed in the **central processing unit**. The computer will then show the results through an output device.

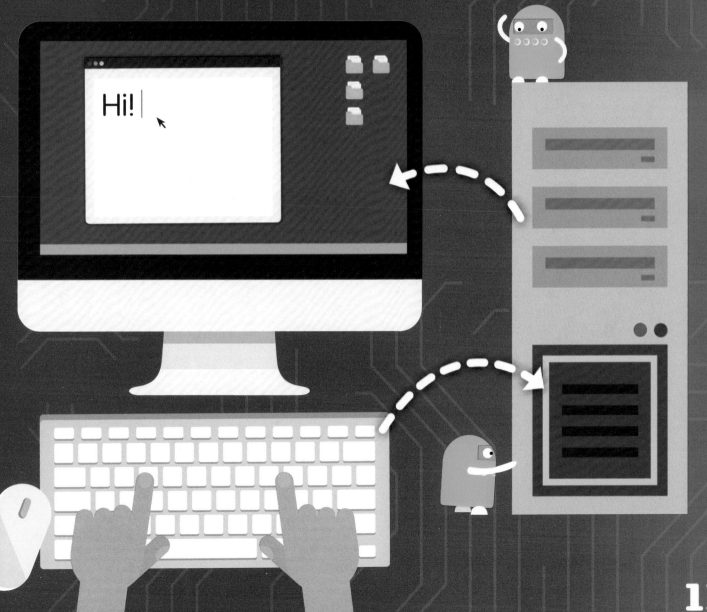

WHAT IS AN ALGORITHM?

An algorithm is a list of instructions that tells a computer what to do. Lots of these lists together make a program. We must give computers clear instructions in the algorithms, so they will understand exactly what to do.

Computers use algorithms to do all sorts of everyday jobs. If you were a computer, this would be the algorithm for brushing your teeth.

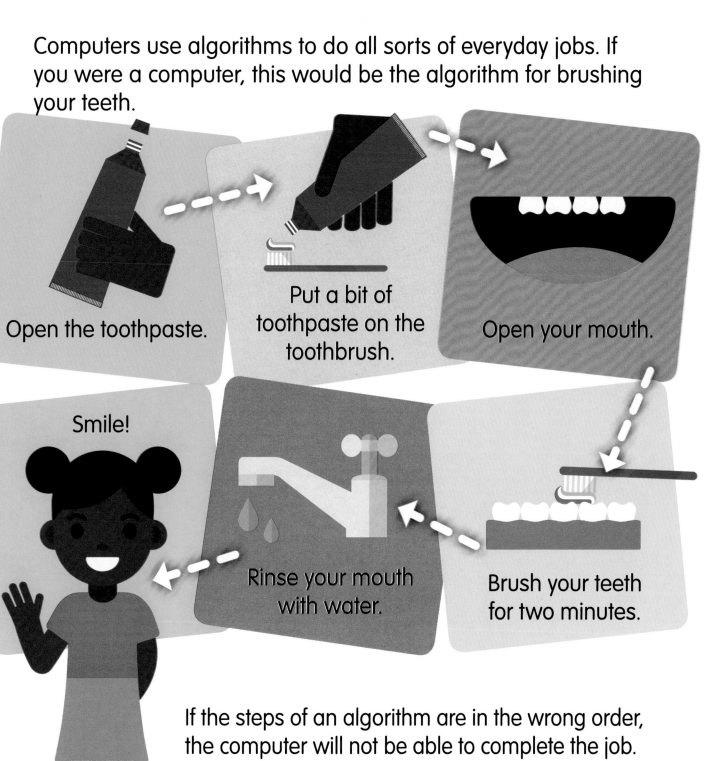

Open the toothpaste.

Put a bit of toothpaste on the toothbrush.

Open your mouth.

Smile!

Rinse your mouth with water.

Brush your teeth for two minutes.

If the steps of an algorithm are in the wrong order, the computer will not be able to complete the job.

COMPUTER
LANGUAGE

Algorithms are written in a language that computers understand, called "code." There are many different computer languages that can look very different from each other, but they all do similar things.

Computer languages use lots of symbols, letters, and numbers that fit together in a special way. Everything must be in the right order, and spelled correctly, so the computer can understand perfectly.

AMAZING MEMORY

Computers can store lots of things in their memory, like videos, music, and games. When we save work on a computer, it is saved as a file.

File

11:24 AM

When we store files, we need to think about the amount of space they take up in the computer's memory. We can measure the size of the file in **bytes**.

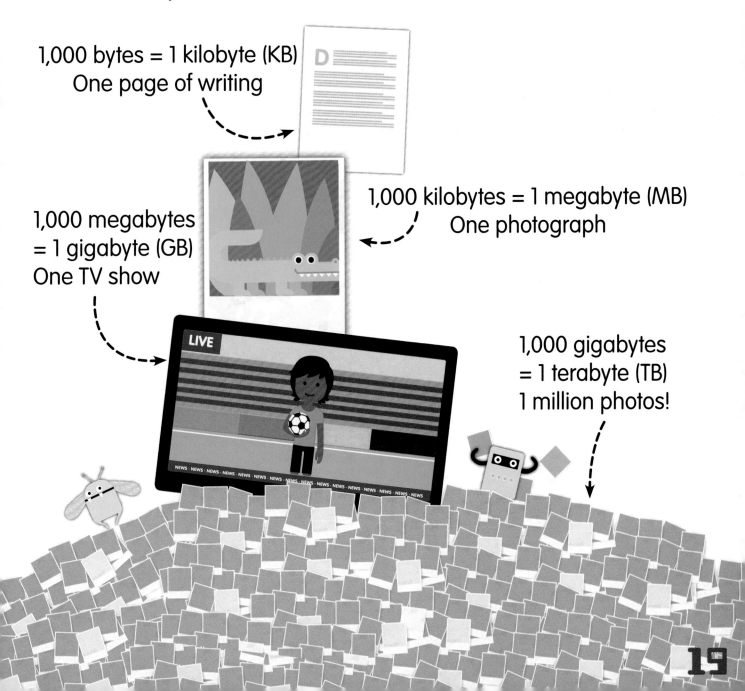

1,000 bytes = 1 kilobyte (KB)
One page of writing

1,000 kilobytes = 1 megabyte (MB)
One photograph

1,000 megabytes
= 1 gigabyte (GB)
One TV show

1,000 gigabytes
= 1 terabyte (TB)
1 million photos!

LIVE

NEWS · NEWS · NEWS · NEWS · NEWS · NEWS · NEWS · NEWS · NEWS · NEWS · NEWS · NEWS · NEWS · NEWS · NEWS · NEWS

PERFECT
PROCESSORS

A computer processor has a very important job to do.
It reads the whole program, which tells it what to do.

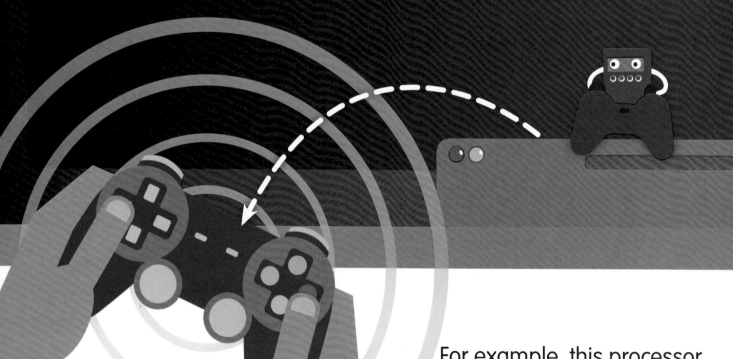

For example, this processor
is sending a message to a
game controller, telling it
to vibrate.

The processor follows algorithms written in code to help it get the job done. Algorithms are very useful, but sometimes they don't work and we need to find out why. Problems with algorithms are called **bugs**.

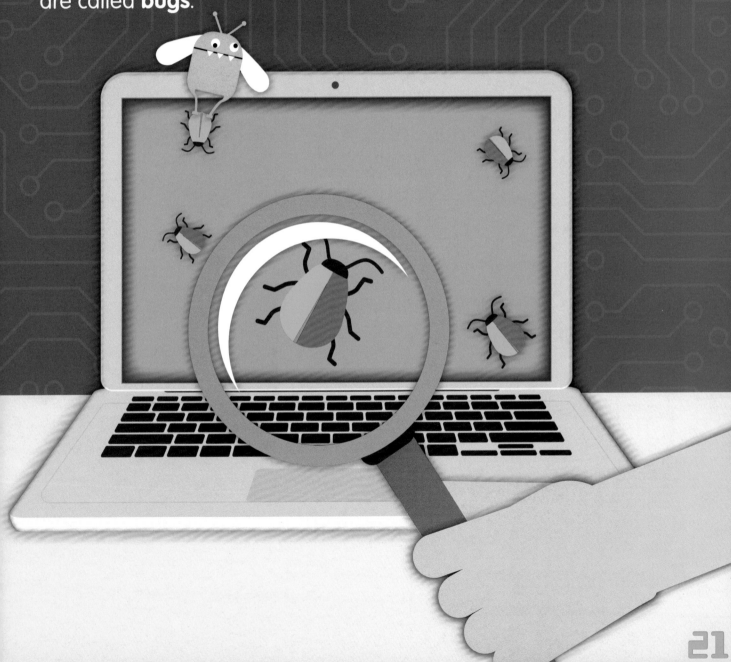

INPUTS AND
OUTPUTS

We use input devices, like keyboards and microphones, to put information into a computer.

Input Devices = − →

Output Devices = - - →

Speaker

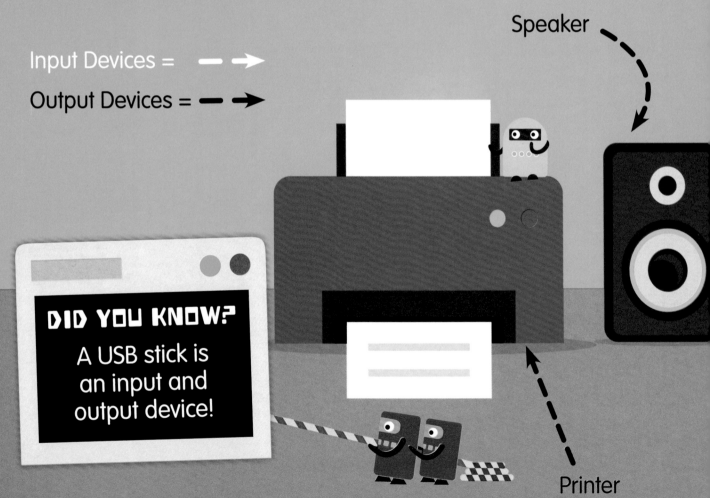

DID YOU KNOW?

A USB stick is an input and output device!

Printer

Output devices give us information, such as words, pictures, or sounds.

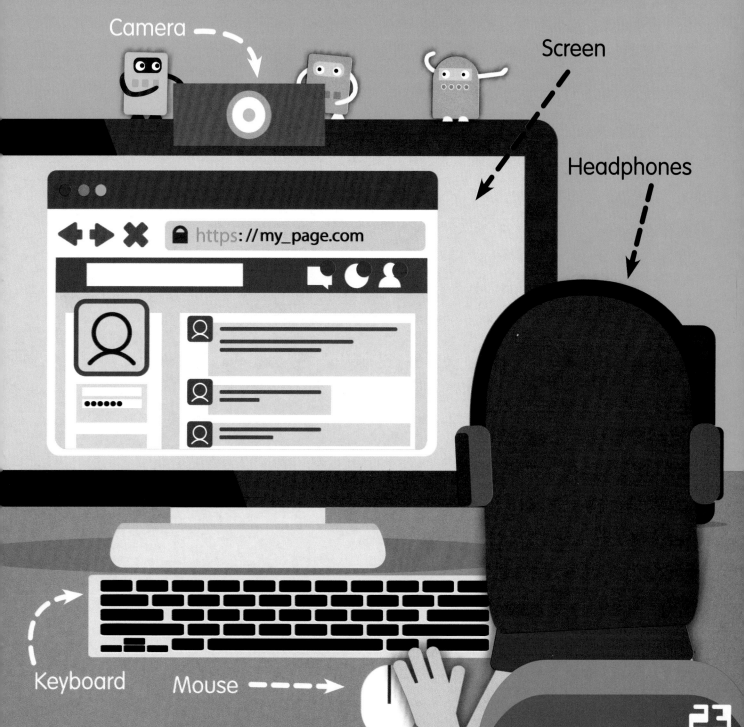

Camera

Screen

Headphones

Keyboard

Mouse

23

GLOSSARY

BUG	an error in code that stops a program from running properly
BYTES	units of computer information
CENTRAL PROCESSING UNIT	part of the computer that follows instructions
COMMUNICATE	share information
DATA	information
ELECTRICITY	energy used to power computers
EMIT	send out information or signals, such as light or sound
INSTRUCTIONS	detailed information explaining how something should be done
MACHINE	a tool or device that performs a task
MODERN	from recent or present times
PERFORM	carry out a job or task
TECHNOLOGY	devices or tools to help us to do something

INDEX